HOW TO SHARE YOUR FAITH WITHOUT FEAR

A BIBLICAL STRATEGY FOR MAKING DISCIPLES

R. JAY WAGGONER

HOW TO SHARE YOUR FAITH WITHOUT FEAR: A BIBLICAL
STRATEGY FOR MAKING DISCIPLES

ISBN-13: 978-1539591511
ISBN-10: 1539591514

This book is dedicated to Dianne and Brittany, whose passion for sharing their faith has touched many lives and often challenged me.

CONTENTS

ACKNOWLEDGMENTS

I am indebted to the many people who have helped make this book a reality. First of all, to my wife and partner in ministry, Dianne, whose encouragement and advice was invaluable as always. I am also grateful for the editorial assistance of Brittany Hochstaetter, Michael Richardson, Gail Smith, Sam Smith, and Jarl Waggoner. Finally, I appreciate the fine folks of Fellowship Baptist Church in Willow Spring, North Carolina, who graciously responded to the message of this book when first preached to them.

INTRODUCTION

Are you intimidated by the idea of sharing your faith? If so, you are not alone. According to recent research, approximately sixty percent of all Christians seldom or never share their faith with others. [1] Is apprehension about sharing your faith a normal experience? Is it due to some spiritual failing on your part? Can it be overcome? If you have ever wrestled with questions like these, this book is for you. The good news is that the fear of sharing your faith can be overcome, even eliminated with the right strategy. Eliminating fear from the equation begins with the right perspective on the problem. Chapters 1 through 4 provide that perspective. Chapters 5 through 7 provide a practical, step-by-step biblical strategy for making disciples that will eliminate the debilitating fear often associated with other methods. Chapter 8 is supplemental and provides further encouragement and help for explaining the gospel message to unbelievers, something that causes great apprehension for many Christians.

---

[1] Revival Outside the Walls, "Get the Facts: Behaviors," rotw.com.

PART 1

PERSPECTIVES ON SHARING YOUR FAITH

1

THE ELEPHANT IN THE LOBBY

Dealing with Fear

During my last year of undergraduate studies, I attended the midweek service of a nearby church where my fiancée was a member. On the first Wednesday I attended, the pastor announced that visitation was the following evening. I envisioned a large group of church members knocking on doors and sharing the gospel message with those they met. So the next evening my future wife and I returned to the church for visitation. We were both somewhat apprehensive, not having previously participated in such a program, but we thought that other, more experienced participants would help us learn the ropes. We were sadly mistaken. Besides the pastor, we were the only ones who showed up for visitation that night.

What we discovered that night is a common malady. Most believers are simply too intimidated to speak to other people about their souls. As Greg Stier has said, "Sharing your faith is a scary prospect. You can lose face and friends as a result of communicating this 'narrow-minded' message of the gospel even when you do so in love. When choosing between being accepted by others and sharing the good news with others too often Christians choose silence. Fear is the biggest culprit that keeps Christians from evangelizing."[2] The failure of Christians to consistently share their faith is widespread. A recent study done by Lifeway Research confirms the extent of the problem. Among those who attend worship once or twice a month, 80 per cent believe they have a responsibility to share their faith with others. However, in the six months previous to the study, a hefty 61 percent revealed that they had not shared their faith with a single person![3]

Certainly, fear is a common reality that we face in life. As part of his creative genius, God gave man the capacity to fear. This emotion serves a valuable and necessary purpose. Otherwise, we would never shy away from any impending danger. However, fear becomes a problem when it interferes with our biblical responsibilities, such as bearing witness to Christ. In such cases, fear is detrimental to our spiritual well-being. The question we must answer is this: What can be done to move past the paralyzing effects of such fear? The answer is not obvious. Let's look at some of the common approaches to dealing with fear of this kind and consider each one.

---

[2] Greg Stier, "Five Reasons Why Christians Struggle to Evangelize," *Christian Post*, August 28, 2012. www. christianpost.com.

[3] Ed Stetzer, "Churchgoers Believe in Sharing Faith, Most Never Do." Lifeway Research, August 13, 2012. Lifewayresearch.com.

The Elephant in the Lobby

SHEER DETERMINATION

One approach is attempting to overcome the fear of sharing our faith by sheer determination. This approach considers fear to be a normal occurrence that must be accepted—perhaps even a God-given reminder that we need to rely on him. Any uneasiness that occurs must be tolerated and God's truth boldly proclaimed in spite of it. This approach is commendable because it takes our biblical responsibilities seriously. It is also doable, as many can attest. However, learning to tolerate fear is an extremely difficult thing to do, and few are able to do so consistently. There is a better solution. We have the spiritual resources to eliminate this kind of fear. It is not something that God has ordained for us to endure. Why would anything that inhibits us from fulfilling our biblical responsibilities be part of God's design? Of course in situations where physical danger and threats of bodily harm are involved, fear would be a natural response. Otherwise, we need to be reminded that the opposite is true. Such fear is not inevitable and in Christ we have the necessary power to eliminate it. "For God has not given us a spirit of fear, but of power and of love and of a sound mind" (2 Tim. 1:7).

Before the birth of my daughter, I refrained from holding babies. They seemed altogether too fragile for me to handle. I never said, "I'm afraid to hold a baby," but I was. However, everything changed the moment my daughter was born. After a brief examination, a nurse handed her to me, and I took her in my arms without a moment's hesitation or fear. What was different this time? Two things were different. First, I had been instructed about how to handle a baby during the childbirth class I had taken with my wife. Second, I was overcome by love for my daughter and desired to be near her. So it is that a sound mind—a mind that is fully informed—along with love that is produced by the Holy Spirit enables us to overcome the fear of sharing our faith. Although the steadfast determination to overcome fear is very likely motivated by love, it is often lacking the definitive knowledge of biblical methodology that is also needed. Without a soundly instructed mind, I may have desired to hold my daughter at birth, but the fear of doing it improperly may have hindered me from doing so. We will examine this truth in more detail in the next chapter.

<h2 align="center">GUILT AS MOTIVATION</h2>

A second and very common approach to the problem assumes that God's people can overcome their fear with the right motivation. A guilty conscience is generally thought to be the best motivation for overcoming fear. Therefore, pastors dutifully preach about the horrors of hell and the believer's responsibility to reach the lost before it is too late. Passages such as the account of the rich man and Lazarus the beggar (Luke 16:19-31), the watchman that doesn't warn a city of the enemy's approach and thus has blood on his hands (Ezek. 33:6), and those referring to the coming Judgment Seat of Christ where rewards may be forfeited (1 Cor. 3:11-15; 2 Cor. 5:10) are used to impale the conscience with guilt. Consequently, the average guilt-ridden Christian sitting in the pew may be prodded into action temporarily. However, this newfound motivation will not last because a guilty conscience is not the solution. Fear will persist in spite of all such preaching, right or wrong. No matter how much guilt people are made to feel, it will not be reason enough for them to consistently confront their fear and share their faith. In the final analysis, the overwhelming majority of believers that are beset by fear will still not share their faith. It's not that they don't care about pleasing God or rescuing the lost. The problem is that their fear persists, alongside any guilt that they feel, and they remain paralyzed by it.

What little value may come from a guilty conscience needs to be tempered by the fact that no one is ever singularly responsible for another person's eternal fate. The Scriptures indicate that all who reject Christ are personally responsible for their own condemnation: "For since the creation of the world His invisible attributes are clearly seen, being understood by the things that are made, even His eternal power and Godhead, so that they are without excuse" (Rom. 1:20). In the end, unbelievers will stand condemned by their own works: "And I saw the dead, small and great, standing before God, and books were opened. And another book was opened, which is the Book of Life. And the dead were judged according to their works, by the things which were written in the books" (Rev. 20:12).

A man once suggested to me that I needed to preach more often on the topic of eternal punishment. In response, I explained that it was my practice to preach through one book of Scripture at a time and that in due time I would come to the subject. Furthermore, I explained that this approach ensures that I give the proper emphasis to every important doctrine in the Bible, but I'm not sure my explanation satisfied him. For many well-meaning believers, the only kind of motivation that will produce dynamic evangelism is guilt. As they see it, if the church fails to win as many souls as it should, it is because God's people are not properly motivated. Their answer is more preaching about the horrors of hell and consequently more guilt about not doing enough to keep people from going there.

Outright Resignation

A third response to the obstacle of fear is complete resignation. The reality is that most Christians have concluded that they simply cannot overcome their fear of speaking to someone about God. Perhaps pastors and missionaries can, but they cannot. Since the fear of sharing our faith is a little embarrassing to admit around other Christians, most simply abstain from sharing their faith without any explanation. On the surface this seems to be simple disobedience in the form of willful omission. The reality of the situation is that the fear of sharing our faith has become the proverbial elephant in the room, or perhaps we should say in the church lobby. Although we realize the elephant is there and that he is a huge problem, we ignore him because we have no idea how to remove him from the room and solve the problem. So, this is not simply a matter of disobedience; it is a matter of hopelessness. Resignation is a very common response to the believer's obligation to share his faith, but unlike the first two approaches, there is no attempt to deal with the problem. Those who are so resigned need to be reminded of two important truths. First, the omission of known responsibilities is sinful and must not be ignored for any reason (James 4:17). And perhaps more important, God would not ask us to do that which we are unable to do. The fact is, we can do all that God requires of us. As Paul said, "I can do all things through Christ who strengthens me" (Phil. 4:13). This being the case, the elephant really can be removed from the lobby. The only hindrance is not knowing how to do it. Once we know how to do it, all we have to do is take the necessary steps.

2

IS THERE A DOCTRINE IN THE HOUSE?

Eliminating Fear

My back had been hurting for weeks. It was nothing new to have some back pain, but this time it was different. The usual remedies helped initially but didn't provide any lasting relief. Stretching, over-the-counter medications, massage, and visits to a chiropractor all helped for a limited time. Within a day or two the pain would return. Finally, it occurred to me that I was treating a symptom—my back pain—without addressing the underlying cause. Something that I was doing or not doing was very bad for my back, and the pain I was experiencing was a red flag. Thinking through what had recently changed about my daily life pinpointed the problem. At a nearby yard sale one Saturday, I had purchased an office chair that was much nicer looking than my old one. Suspecting it might be the cause of my back pain, I switched it out for my old chair, and my back pain promptly went away. Treating my pain had not produced a lasting solution because it was only a symptom of the underlying problem.

The fear we encounter when we attempt to share our faith is a very real and stubborn obstacle, but it too is only a symptom. Any attempt to overcome our fear without addressing the underlying cause will prove frustrating at best. Fear will continue to plague us until we deal with the root cause. When we do, we will be freed from the clutches of fear. Yes, as unlikely as it may seem, it is as simple as that. The fear of sharing our faith can be eliminated. All that is necessary is to address the cause. This can be done by following a simple, but effective plan of treatment.

AN ACCURATE DIAGNOSIS

After the fall, Adam hid in shame. When God approached him, Adam explained that he had hidden himself in fear because he was naked (Gen. 3:8-10). Adam's fear was caused by his shame. There was no shame in his nakedness prior to his sin. Previously, he had enjoyed a perfect and untainted relationship with God. Now his sin and the shame of it had impacted that perfect fellowship and left fear in its wake. This is the first mention of fear in the Bible, and it is clearly the result of Adam's sin. Fear is always the result of some underlying and identifiable cause. When a part of our brain called the amygdala reacts to a stressful situation, it triggers the release of adrenaline into the bloodstream. This is often referred to as the "fight or flight" response. In some circumstances it is beneficial because it enables us to respond physically to a threat. In other cases, it is a bothersome symptom of misguided thinking. When it comes to the fear of sharing our faith, the diagnosis is clearly that of a faulty perspective. Since we have found sharing our faith to be stressful in the past, the very thought of doing it again evokes fear. In such cases it takes the truth to set us free.

My daughter was afraid of wolves when she was a preschooler. She had watched some terrorizing scene about a pack of wolves on TV and was sure that they posed a threat to her well-being every night as soon as the sun went down. It took quite a while to convince her that the nearest wolves lived many hundreds of miles away from where we lived. Once she came to understand that there were no wolves nearby to worry about, her fear went away. Her fear had been based on a faulty concept—that wolves were present in her environment. Likewise, there is some faulty concept or perspective that causes us to fear sharing our faith with another person. This underlying cause must be identified and its resulting perspective corrected before fear can be eliminated.

Unfortunately, many believers have been conditioned to think that evangelism is aggressively and indiscriminately confronting as many people as possible with the gospel message. After all, time is short, and hell is hot. The problem with this approach to evangelism is that the vast majority of believers are not comfortable using it. The very thought of confronting someone, especially a stranger, with the gospel is terrifying to them. The unfortunate fact is that this concept is often considered the singular definition of evangelism. Joseph Aldrich aptly described the problem this

way: "Research indicates that only 10 percent of believers are gifted to share Christ using the methods presented in almost 100 percent of the classes on personal
evangelism."[4] Granted, a few will be able to use a confrontational approach to evangelism. However, the fact
remains that most will not even attempt it. If the majority of believers are to be freed from the fear that
inhibits them from evangelizing the lost, this widespread and faulty perspective needs to be corrected.
There is another model for sharing our faith that will
enable anyone to effectively evangelize.

A GOOD PROGNOSIS

Before we move on to the biblical model that should
shape our perspective, we need to understand that we
have the spiritual resources necessary for eliminating
the fear of sharing our faith. The prognosis is good.
Fear need not hinder us. Note first that the issue of
whether or not we can share our faith effectively has
been settled. Paul writes in Acts 1:8, "But you shall receive power when the Holy Spirit has come upon you;
and you shall be witnesses to me in Jerusalem, and in
all Judea and Samaria, and to the end of the earth."
Immediately before his ascension Jesus promised his
disciples that they would receive power after the Holy
Spirit came upon them. The word translated "power"
refers to raw power or strength. It is a word that has

---

4 Joseph C. Aldrich, *Gentle Persuasion* (Portland, OR: Multnomah
Press, 1988), 10.

come over into the English language in our word *dyna-mite*. What Jesus meant was that the Holy Spirit from the Day of Pentecost onward would enable all believers to do what God required of them. Moreover, Acts 1:8 specifically mentions the fact that those so empowered would as a result be his witnesses throughout Jerusalem, Judea, Samaria, and to the ends of the earth. The conclusion is obvious: every believer in Jesus Christ has the ability to share his or her faith. Paul used the same Greek word as Luke did in Acts 1:8 when he reminded Timothy of his spiritual power: "For God has not given us a spirit of fear, but of power and of love and of a sound mind" (2 Tim. 1:7). The Holy Spirit who indwells us is most certainly not the source of fear but rather the opposite—the source of power.

Having the ability to share our faith is an essential spiritual resource, but the motivation to do so is also needed. Paul identified the necessary motivation for overcoming fear in his words to Timothy. Love is that motivation. "Love" in the original is *agape*. It refers to Godlike love—ultimate sacrificial love. It is our love for God that is meant. "We love him because He first loved us" (1 John 4:19). The ability to love God is supplied by the Holy Spirit as we allow him to direct us. "The fruit of the Spirit is love" (Gal. 5:22). Again, the prognosis is good.

Finally, Paul adds the third and final resource of a "sound mind" to his list of spiritual resources needed to overcome fear. Spiritual ability and the right motivation are still dependent on our understanding of what God wants us to do and how he wants us to do it. Therefore, a "sound mind" is also needed. The Holy Spirit has supplied us with this resource as well (2 Tim. 1:7). The limiting factor has been an absence of sound teaching. Sound minds still need sound teaching before proper perspectives can be formed.

THE RIGHT PRESCRIPTION

Finally, the right prescription in regard to sharing our faith is crucial. Without the proper prescription, we cannot possibly treat the problem, and unless we treat the underlying problem, the symptom of fear will persist. Without a doubt, the right prescription is a biblical perspective. It is born out of a sound mind that is directed by the Holy Spirit and focused on the Scriptures.

There are multiple examples in the Bible of people sharing their faith, but there is no singular model or methodology employed. Some methods are more assertive and impersonal than others, and some believers may gravitate to them. However, there is among these examples a relational model that can be identified and easily employed by any believer. The existence of this relational model is often overlooked, but it is clearly present in the Scriptures, and it will alleviate the symptom of fear.

The relational model for sharing our faith is stretched out over much of the New Testament, but the foundational underpinning comes from the words of Jesus in Matthew 22. Jesus said to a man who questioned him, "You shall love the Lord your God with all your heart, with all your soul, and with all your mind. This is the first and great commandment. And the second is like it: You shall love your neighbor as yourself" (Matt. 22:37-39). These words provide us with an overview of all that we will explore in detail going forward. When questioned about what was the greatest commandment, Jesus replied that man's obligation was to first love God and then to love his neighbor. The two concepts are connected. We cannot love God and not love our neighbors. Love requires that we give something to another person. Loving someone is where we begin the task of sharing our faith.

When Doug Meland of Wycliffe Bible Translators, along with his wife, moved into a village of Brazil's Fulnino Indians, he was referred to by the Indians as "the white man." It was not a simple descriptive term. It was, rather, a derogatory one since "white men" had exploited them in the past. However, after Meland learned their language and began to help the people by supplying medical assistance, they began calling him "the respectable white man." In time, as the Melands began adapting to the customs of the people and gained greater acceptance, Doug was called "the white Indian." Finally, one day as Doug was washing the dirty foot of an injured Fulnino boy, he overheard an onlooker say, "Whoever heard of a white man washing an Indian's foot before? Certainly this man is from God!"

From that day forward, Doug was referred to as "the man God sent us."[5]

Sharing our faith is simply a matter of loving people, and loving people is a natural consequence of loving God. The only natural thing about aggressively confronting unbelievers with the gospel, especially total strangers, is that it evokes fear.

---

[5] Paul Lee Tan, *Encyclopedia of 7700 Illustrations* (Rockville, MD, Assurance Publishers, 1979), 3201.

3

THE GREAT CONFUSION

Clarifying Our Call

Recently, I heard that a well-known Christian author was preaching at a nearby church. Not having many such opportunities, I went to hear him speak. His text was Mark 16:15: "Go into all the world and preach the gospel to every creature." In the course of his message, he said that the Lord is still telling each of us to go into all the world and preach the gospel to every creature. Then after mentioning that he had visited well over one hundred countries, incredibly, he asked us, "How many countries have you been in?" I still find it hard to believe he actually meant what he said. Are we really supposed to understand the Great Commission in this way? Perhaps he was trying to say that believers are responsible for telling as many people as possible about Christ. This would be a more credible view. It is certainly the more prevalent one. However, either way, his interpretation is suspect. In fact, it is likely to cause discouragement rather than motivate anyone. When believers are saddled with such a burdensome task as many people make evangelism out to be, many give up on sharing their faith altogether. They conclude that although others may be up to the task, they certainly are not. So they resign themselves to second-class status as Christians. It is a shame when this happens. Rather than thinking they are useless due to a false standard, believers should see themselves and their contributions—whatever they are—as important parts of God's program.

God's program in this age—our primary responsibility—is readily acknowledged by virtually everyone who names the name of Christ. We refer to it as the Great Commission. Mark 16:15 summarizes it, but Matthew 28:19-20 provides the details of our commission: "Go therefore, and make disciples of all nations, baptizing them in the name of the Father and of the Son and of the Holy Spirit." On the surface our calling seems clear in this very familiar passage. Christians hardly give it a second thought. However, in reality, confusion reigns. Without much thought at all, most believers impose some inaccurate idea or ideas upon these verses. The most common fallacy involves equating the Great Commission solely with eliciting decisions for Christ—often called "soul winning." When God's Word is misunderstood in such a way, again, discouragement is often the outcome. Then, once discouragement has gained a foothold, resignation soon follows. As a result, the Great Commission, although acknowledged by all, is seldom a vibrant reality in anyone's life. This does not need to be the case. Since the problem stems from a misunderstanding of our commission, the key to enthusiastic involvement is simply the reverse: the proper understanding of it and what it requires. We need to clarify our calling. Doing so will help us eliminate any doubts we may have about our ability to confidently share our faith. Two important truths need to be embraced in order for us to clarify our calling.

WE CAN'T REACH EVERYONE

The first truth we must embrace is that we do not have to share our faith with everyone. The key element in this regard is understanding to whom the Great Commission was addressed. The assumption is often made that the responsibility was given to individual Christians. The conclusion that is most often drawn from this assumption is that individuals are obligated to share the gospel message in a comprehensive manner. As we have seen, the same conclusion is often drawn from Mark 16:15: "Go into all the world and preach the gospel to every creature." So, does the Great Commission require that we force-feed the gospel message to everyone we meet? Are we to wedge the gospel into every conversation, even the most casual ones? If the Great Commission was given to individual believers, then the comprehensive confrontation of everyone we meet with the gospel is indeed required, but the Great Commission was not addressed to the individual Christian.

The problem associated with seeing the Great Commission as an individual responsibility is that such a view saddles us with a difficult and burdensome task that sets us up for failure and discouragement. For example, an evangelist with whom I have often dined at local restaurants always makes it a point to share the gospel message with the waiter or waitress. I do not. I'm simply not comfortable taking such a direct approach with someone I do not know in such a public manner. I will admit that I have admired my friend's ability to speak to anyone and everyone about their need of the Lord, but should I emulate him? Are he and those like him the only ones fulfilling the Great Commission? If so, then I would be a failure for not taking the same assertive approach. However, not having the means to change my personality, I would be tempted to give up on evangelism altogether rather than violate my basic nature. Unfortunately, many Christians find themselves in just such a situation. However, this does not need to be the case. Again, the Great Commission was not addressed to the individual believer at all.

If not to individual Christians, then, to whom was the Great Commission given? Actually, it was given to the church as a whole, the entire universal body of Christ, and not individual believers. When Christ gave the Great Commission, he was speaking to a large group of believers just before his ascension. It was his last message to the group as a whole and to the apostles in particular—those who would soon become the foundation of the church (Eph. 2:19-20). So the Great Commission is the commission of the church given in advance of its founding. It is the church as a whole that is commissioned to carry the gospel to all nations. Individual members of the universal church all play a role in this commission but are not individually dispatched to fulfill the commission all by themselves. If that were the case, then baptizing converts and teaching each one of them would also be the individual's responsibility rather than the responsibility of a local church.

Of course, there is an obvious connection between the church's commission and the individual's responsibility since the church is made up of individual believers. Individuals, as well as local churches as a whole, have to be committed to and focused on the Great Commission. However, the Great Commission is a corporate responsibility. Everyone has a part to play in fulfilling the commission, but not everyone has the same responsibility. Fortunately, the Great Commission does not require a cookie-cutter approach. The Great Commission is not a method; it is the commission of the church. Each individual member has his or her own unique way of being a witness to the world. Some are even suited for confrontational evangelism. However, equating the Great Commission with a singular assertive method is misguided and even detrimental. As already mentioned, viewing the confrontational method as the essence of the individual's obligation and saddling everyone with such a burden is counterproductive. It will only set up the majority of believers for failure. Discouragement and possibly the abandonment of any effort at all to reach the lost may follow. We must not lose sight of the fact that all believers are already a witness. Jesus did not tell his disciples to "be" a witness in Acts 1:8. He said they "would be" witnesses. The truth is that every believer in Christ is a witness of his grace in one way or another, to one person or another, by words or deeds, somehow or in some way. Somewhere we all fit into the corporate witness of the church. We do not have to reach everyone, but we should be involved in the overall process.

WE CAN MAKE DISCIPLES

The second truth we need to embrace about our calling is that we are to be actively involved in the process of making disciples. The main verb in Matthew 28:19-20 is translated "make disciples." Although it is translated "teach" in the KJV, it is the verb form of the word *disciple* as the NKJV correctly translates. This is clearly a broad obligation that involves much more than merely eliciting decisions. Indeed, making disciples is a much more comprehensive obligation. The two participles that follow the main verb—"baptizing" and "teaching"—indicate the necessary methodology required in order to make disciples. These two participles along with the main verb, all of which are present tense, indicate that the Great Commission involves a multifaceted and ongoing process—the process of making disciples. Obviously, this process is best accomplished in the context of a local church because it is the church that was commissioned. This being the case, individual believers cannot fulfill the Great Commission on their own but should enter into the broader process at one point or another.

The Great Confusion

The person God uses to bring an individual to faith in Christ usually does not complete the task of teaching that person all that is required of disciples. As Paul wrote, "For though you might have ten thousand instructors in Christ, yet you do not have many fathers; for in Christ Jesus I have begotten you through the gospel" (1 Cor. 4:15). Multiple "instructors" enter into the discipleship process sometime after the initial conversion and teach the disciple some aspect of God's truth. Therefore, adopting other believers as disciples is just as much a part of the Great Commission as birthing new believers. Both are important. Equating the Great Commission with the making of converts and failing to comprehend the entire scope of the obligation is a severely limited view of the Great Commission. In such a view those who help complete the task are not considered a part of the commission. So, all are pressured to win souls. In fact, some are pressured to abandon what they are doing well (edifying other believers) in order to do what they don't do well (make converts). Both are necessary. Both are part of the Great Commission, and no one's role should be disparaged. Those who are better at edification should endeavor to learn from those who excel at evangelism rather than give up on evangelism altogether. Moreover, those who excel at evangelism should realize that not everyone in the body will be as drawn to evangelism as they are, but those who are not are also involved in the work of the Great Commission. Mutual respect and understanding leads to maximum involvement in the making of disciples. Everyone should have a sense of his or her purpose and importance in the overall process. Unfortunately, not everyone does. Allen's email message sent to me after I had preached on the Great Commission highlights the problem.

> So often it seems you hear from pulpits that unless you are winning souls to Christ you aren't really fulfilling your mission as a Christian. If I wasn't confronting people … then I was a failure. I know that for decades I led a defeated Christian life where I felt inadequate because my personality didn't lend itself to one-on-one witnessing. Therefore, if I didn't have opportunities to go to the mission field, and I wasn't involved in one-on-one witnessing, I must not have much value to the cause of Christ. I can only imagine how many others feel worthless in a similar way. It took many years for me to figure it out on my own. It was encouraging to see teaching and making disciples as real parts of the Great Commission, and I thank you for making it so clear this morning.

When famed English architect Christopher Wren was overseeing the construction of St. Paul's Cathedral in London, some of the workers were interviewed by a journalist who asked various workers what they were doing. One replied that he was cutting stone for three shillings a day. Another said he was putting in ten hours a day doing construction work. A third man offered a completely different perspective. He said, "I am helping Christopher Wren build the greatest cathedral in Great Britain for the glory of God."[6] Likewise, every Christian should see his or her ministry involvement, whatever it is, as part of the Great Commission of reaching lost souls for Christ. That commission is the most important endeavor in human history. It is worth noting that it is also the most successful endeavor in history. According to recent statistics, Christianity currently has more adherents than any other religion on the planet.[7] It is our privilege to be a part of God's program in this age—whatever role we have in that program—and it is not in any way insignificant.

---

[6] Robert Morgan, *Nelson's Complete Book of Stories, Illustrations & Quotes* (Nashville: Thomas Nelson Publishers, 2000), 800.

[7] Adherents.com (accessed 2005).

4

METHODOLOGY MATTERS

Evaluating Our Methods

Charles Caldwell was a Civil War veteran, lay preacher, state senator, and lawyer of some renown who practiced law at the turn of the twentieth century in my hometown. "Old Charley," as he was called, was perhaps best known for his wit and eloquence in the courtroom. On many occasions it was standing-room only in the courtroom when he was scheduled to address the court. On one occasion an opposing lawyer who had just lost a case to "Old Charley" became so enraged at his courtroom antics that he challenged Charley to a duel. The opposing lawyer happened to have a head of thick red hair. In stark contrast, "Old Charley" didn't have a hair on his head. He was bald as a cue ball. After the challenge was issued to him, Charley asked for permission to address the court on the subject of dueling. The judge, confident Charley would diffuse the whole situation, granted his request. With great eloquence, Charley reviewed the history of dueling, stressing its evils and ending with an explanation that the challenged party always had the right to choose the time, the place, and the weapons to be used. Upon finishing his lecture, "Old Charley" reportedly removed his coat, rolled up his sleeves, and turned to his challenger, stating, "The time, sir, is now. The place, sir, is this courtroom. The weapons, sir, are pulling hair. Make ready, sir."[8] Charley's response to the challenge was unusual, but it achieved the desired effect — the duel never took place.

The way in which we tackle any endeavor makes a world of difference. It is no different when it comes to sharing our faith with unbelievers. Although the Great Commission is much broader than the initial making of a disciple, it begins there. This initial aspect of disciple making is what we call evangelism. A number of evangelistic methods can be identified in the New Testament. Three are worthy of our consideration. The method we choose to employ is vitally important.

THE METHOD OF PROCLAMATION

One method of evangelism that is unmistakable in the New Testament is proclamation. This method is associated with preaching. In fact, the word translated

---

[8] Howard B. Lee, *The Burning Springs and Other Tales of the Little Kanawha* (Parsons, WV: McClain Publishing Company, 1968), 123.

"preach" in the New Testament means "announce publicly" or "proclaim aloud." This is the word Peter used to describe the command God had given him and the other disciples in regard to making Christ known to the world (Acts 10:42). It is also the method employed by the apostles immediately after the baptism of the Spirit on the Day of Pentecost: "And when this sound occurred, the multitude came together, and were confused, because everyone heard them speak in his own language. ... And Peter, standing up with the eleven, raised his voice and said to them, 'Men of Judea and all who dwell in Jerusalem, let this be known to you, and heed my words'" (Acts 2:6, 14). As a result of Peter's preaching, about three thousand came to faith in Christ (Acts 2:41). Later, Peter again preached to a crowd, and many more professed faith in Christ (Acts 4:4). Throughout the history of the church, proclamation has been utilized as a successful method of reaching the lost. From Peter, to George Whitefield, to John Wesley, to Dwight Moody, to Billy Graham, proclamation, the preaching of the Word, has been used of God to bring thousands to faith in Christ. To a great many Christians over a great many years, evangelism has been synonymous with holding a preaching service featuring the preaching of a fiery evangelist. Unbelievers are simply invited to attend, and the rest is left to the preaching of the gospel and the work of the Spirit.

Sometimes lost in this whole concept of proclamation as evangelism is that something or someone must convince unbelievers to submit themselves to the formal preaching of the gospel. In the case of Peter's first sermon after Pentecost, it was the tongues phenomenon (Acts 2:6). In the second instance, it was the very public healing of the lame man in the temple area (Acts 3:1-11). In every other case down to the last time you or I saw a person make a public profession of faith, someone had a hand in getting that person under the preaching of the gospel. The proclamation of the gospel was simply the last part of a process involving events orchestrated by God, including the influence of concerned believers. Behind every person who has ever walked an aisle to receive Christ is a significant backstory. So, the public proclamation of the gospel alone cannot be thought of as the standard methodology for evangelism. At best, it is part of a broader process that requires significant relationships being in place beforehand.

THE CONFRONTATIONAL METHOD

A second methodology is often called "confrontational evangelism." By confrontational it is meant that unbelievers are personally confronted with the gospel. The basic idea is to clearly and forcefully deliver the message of salvation. The emphasis is on making a rational argument for the person to receive Christ. "Soul win-

Methodology Matters

ning" is the traditional term for this method. More recently it has been labeled "confrontational evangelism."[9] The venue varies from knocking on doors to street preaching. Although friends and family members are not excluded, it is the impersonal evangelizing of strangers that is emphasized. Anyone and everyone is approached indiscriminately without the benefit of a preexisting relationship. The question is not whether this method can be used to reach people for Christ. It can and has. The problem with this method is that the majority of Christians are not comfortable with this type of approach.[10] It requires the ability to approach strangers and win them over to Christ. There is nothing subtle about confrontational evangelism. It is not necessarily rude, but it is straightforward. The question we must ask is whether or not this is the basic New Testament model. If it is, then all Christians should learn to confront the lost, whether they are comfortable doing so or not. Regrettably, this is what some believe.

Jon Speed has made the case for confrontational evangelism being the standard biblical method. He asserts that 86.5 percent of the evangelistic encounters

---

[9] Jon Speed, *Evangelism in the New Testament* (Lost Cause Ministries, 2008), 7.

[10] Joseph C. Aldrich, *Gentle Persuasion*, 10.

found in the Gospels are encounters with strangers.[11] If his calculations are correct, then perhaps confrontational evangelism is the primary biblical model of evangelism. However, a closer look at Speed's list of encounters leaves his argument on shaky ground. When accounts of healing done by Jesus that do not specifically include any mention of personal salvation are removed from Speed's list, the percentage drops significantly. Furthermore, many of what Speed calls "stranger encounters" clearly deal with matters of discipleship rather than evangelism. A good example is the Sermon on the Mount (Matt. 5:1–7:29), which Speed lists as a "stranger encounter." Dropping these encounters from the list brings the percentage of "stranger encounters" down to around 50 percent of Speed's total sample.[12] Other references in his list of encounters could be labeled relational just as easily as confrontational, and this would further reduce the percentage of "stranger encounters." For example, although a number of "sinners" met Jesus for the first time at the dinner Matthew hosted, they most certainly had a prior relationship with Matthew (Mark 2:14-17). Another example to consider is that much of Jesus' preaching to the crowds included a relational element as well, since many followed him about on a regular basis. All considered, it is evident that Speed's argument at best is not conclusive. Although, confron-

---

[11] Jon Speed, *Evangelism in the New Testament*, 12.

[12] Ibid., 45-46.

tational evangelism is a viable method that has been used successfully countless times over the years, it is clearly not the singular New Testament model of evangelism.

THE RELATIONAL METHOD

A third evangelistic method may be called "relational evangelism." It has also been labeled "lifestyle evangelism" and "friendship evangelism." The contention of this book is that "relational evangelism" is the foundational or primary biblical model. To make this point, we have to again consider the Great Commission. At first glance the Great Commission might seem to support a confrontational and necessarily impersonal methodology: "Go therefore, and make disciples of all nations" (Matt. 20:19). Unfortunately, this very common understanding of the Great Commission is based more on what has been said about the Great Commission than what it actually says. When we take a careful look at the Great Commission, the relational aspect becomes obvious.

There are four levels of relationship involved in fulfilling the Great Commission. First, those of us going into the world already have a relationship with Christ. Second, we develop relationships with other people we meet. Third, we introduce those we meet to Christ. If they embrace him through faith, a three-way relationship is established. In many cases, the people we meet already know Christ, and we assume the part of a disciple maker in a new three-way relationship with them. Finally, as disciple makers, we bring those to whom we minister into a relationship with the church, where they are baptized and taught. This means that we have now established a fourth level of relationship. Without a doubt, the Great Commission is a relational model.

As we have noted in the previous chapter, the Great Commission is about making disciples and not simply eliciting decisions from unbelievers. Therefore every evangelistic method, in order to be true to the Great Commission, needs to culminate in the making of disciples. Unfortunately, both "proclamation" and "confrontational evangelism" tend to see discipleship as a separate function. Quite possibly this is because discipleship is by definition relational. On the other hand, the relational approach to evangelism integrates seamlessly with discipleship. In fact, it is in reality the same thing. So, it seems logical to view the relational model as the foundational model for sharing our faith. Whether we are introducing unbelievers to Christ or furthering the edification of fellow disciples, relationships are at the center of the process. This is why the relational model is both easier and far less intimidating for the majority of believers.

Our duty to make disciples by sharing our faith can be illustrated by the well-known board game Sorry! In this game that pits four players against each other, each player must move four pawns around a square track. The number of spaces a pawn may be moved on a player's turn is determined by drawing cards that specify the number of spaces an individual pawn may advance. The object of the game is to be the first player to move all four pawns completely around the square track, advancing them into their home space at the end. Of course, there are many pitfalls along the way, including being sent back to the start when an opponent's pawn lands on your occupied space. Disregarding the competitive aspect of Sorry! we can conceive of our responsibility to make disciples by thinking of a similar process. We obviously encounter far more than four people in our lives, but however many there are, we must attempt to move them closer to Christ. Some of those we meet will be unbelievers. We should attempt to bring them into a relationship with Christ. Others we meet are already believers. We should nudge them toward greater Christlikeness. In the end, we should seek to share our faith with every person in our sphere of acquaintances.

PART 2

PLANNING TO SHARE YOUR FAITH

5

THE RELATIONSHIP LANDSCAPE

Becoming Intentional

An often-told anecdote recounts the story of a traveler who passed by a barn that had a number of arrows protruding from one side. Each arrow was perfectly centered in the bull's-eye of a separate target painted on the side of the barn. Impressed by the archer's apparent skill, the traveler stopped at the farmhouse nearby to congratulate the farmer on his fine marksmanship. Upon receiving the compliment, the farmer laughed and told the passerby that a local boy had shot each arrow into the side of the barn at random and then afterwards carefully painted a bull's-eye around each arrow. Although impressive in appearance, there was absolutely no marksmanship involved. This is much like the approach employed to reach unbelievers by many well-meaning Christians: Gospel arrows are launched indiscriminately in hope of hitting a target. Undoubtedly, God can use haphazard efforts to reach unbelievers, and he sometimes does. However, it is foolish to believe this is the best way to go about making disciples. Random, impersonal efforts to reach others for Christ often produce the very anxiety that is our greatest obstacle to sharing our faith. A much more intentional approach is needed.

As we have previously determined, it is possible for all believers to overcome the fear of sharing their faith and fulfill their part in the Great Commission. We have also explored in general terms how to share our faith without fear, but specifics are needed. A clear-cut plan must be implemented. Those who favor confrontational evangelism often criticize those who are not confrontational of being passive. Undoubtedly, there are many who rely solely on setting a good example and hoping that others will notice, but passivity is not a plan. Admittedly, the relational model involves a more deliberate process than the confrontational approach, but it is not passive. It is a deliberate, step-by-step approach. The process begins with becoming intentional about making disciples. In other words, we need to target the individuals we have the best opportunity to reach and focus our time, energy, and resources on sharing our faith with them. There are two specific ways to achieve this intentionality, and they comprise the first two steps in sharing our faith without fear.

INVENTORY YOUR RELATIONSHIPS

The first way to achieve intentionality is to take an inventory of our existing relationships. Everyone has an existing social network or sphere of relationships. Those who are active on social media can begin there, but a comprehensive inventory of relationships will need to be taken. Most will probably discover their network of relationships include far more individuals than first thought. Remember, it is not only close friends who make up our social network. We all have many casual acquaintances we should not forget to include in our inventory from the waiter at our favorite restaurant to the neighbor down the street.

It is this social network that will provide us with the best setting for sharing our faith and give us the greatest opportunity to successfully impact others for Christ.

Our family is obviously the best starting point for our inventory. They provide the best opportunity for us to share our faith. The Scriptures offer many varied examples of family-centered evangelism.

- Upon being introduced to Jesus, Andrew immediately went to his brother Simon (Peter) and shared the news with him. "He first found his own brother Simon, and said to him. 'We have found the Messiah' (which is translated, the Christ)" (John 1:41).

- The nobleman whose son Jesus healed believed and then through his testimony, his household followed. "And he himself believed, and his whole household" (John 4:53).

- Cornelius called together his family and friends to hear Peter (Acts 10:24), and they all became believers. "While Peter was still speaking these words, the Holy Spirit fell upon all those who heard the word" (Acts 10:44).

- Lydia's household believed and were baptized with her after she accepted Christ (Acts 16:14-15).

- The keeper of the prison in Philippi and his household presents a similar case. "Then he called for a light, ran in, and fell down trembling before Paul and Silas. And he brought them out and said, 'Sirs, what must I do to be saved?' So they said, 'Believe on the Lord Jesus Christ, and you will be saved, you and your household.' Then they spoke the word of the Lord to him and to all who were in his house. And he took them the same hour of the night and washed their stripes. And immediately he and all his family were baptized. Now when he had brought them into his house, he sat food before them; and he rejoiced, having believed in God with all his household" (Acts 16:29-34).

- Finally, Crispus is another example: "Then Crispus, the ruler of the synagogue, believed on the Lord with all his household" (Acts 18:8).

Interestingly, research indicates that if the father is the first in the family to become a Christian, there is a 93 percent chance everyone in the household will follow him.[13] Another survey of believers discovered that 67 percent were initially influenced by a family

---

[13] Bob Horner, Ron Ralston, and David Sunde, *The Promise Keeper at Work* (Colorado Springs: Focus on the Family, 1996), 111.

member.[14] Obviously, our own family is the best place to begin the process of sharing our faith.

An inventory of relationships should also include our friends. Again, examples can be found in the Scriptures.

- Phillip was instrumental in bringing his friend and fellow Galilean, Nathaniel, to Jesus (John 1:45).

- Perhaps Jesus was directed to Philip by Andrew and Peter, who already knew him since they were from the same town (John 1:43-44).

- Jesus heavily impacted the lives of Mary, Martha, and Lazarus of Bethany, who were all close personal friends (Luke 10:38-42; John 11:1-44).

Once again, current research provides confirmation. According to one source 80 percent of those who trust Christ and remain members of a local church are led to the Lord by a friend.[15] Another source places friends second only to family members in importance when it comes to who makes the initial contact.[16]

The last category of relationships we should inventory is our neighbors. Neighbors include everyone who

---

[14] Ron Johnson, Joseph Hinkle, and Charles Lowry, *Oikos, A Practical Approach to Family Evangelism* (Nashville: Broadman, 1982), 54.

[15] Joseph Aldrich, *Gentle Persuasion*, 98.

[16] Johnson, Hinkle, and Lowry, *Oikos, A Practical Approach to Family Evangelism*, 54.

is not already part of the first two categories. Andrew and Peter may or may not have been friends with Philip, but they were definitely neighbors: "Now Phillip was from Bethsaida, the city of Andrew and Peter" (John 1:43-44). The best illustration of our duty to love our neighbors comes from the account of the Good Samaritan (Luke 10:25-37). Jesus used the term *neighbor* to include everyone except ourselves in speaking of our duty to love others (Matt. 22:39). Although we have already separated out family and friends, we still have an almost unlimited supply of neighbors to reach.

EXTEND YOUR NETWORK

Once we have inventoried all our existing relationships, we need to consider extending our social network to those we do not already know. There are plenty of people we encounter in the course of everyday life that could be incorporated into our network with a little effort. Most of us have more time and opportunities than we realize to develop new relationships. Therefore, we need to carefully identify any potential relationships that can be added to our existing ones.

The Jews had excluded the Samaritans from their social network, but Jesus went out of his way to reach one key Samaritan woman. "He left Judea and departed again to Galilee. But He needed to go through Samaria" (John 4:3-4). His journey to Samaria was intentional. There he met a Samaritan woman at the well of Jacob who recognized him as the Messiah (John 4:3-

The Relationship Landscape

26). Consequently, her faith led many others to Christ. "And many of the Samaritans of that city believed in Him because of the word of the woman who testified, 'He told me all that I ever did'" (John 4:39). All of this Jesus intended, but his disciples didn't see the opportunity. As the crowd of Samaritans who had heard the woman's testimony approached, he admonished the disciples, "Behold, I say to you, lift up your eyes and look at the fields, for they are already white for harvest!" (John 4:35). So, too, we ought to lift up our eyes and see the opportunities.

When Barnabas and Paul (Saul) were called to missionary work, they were intentional about their destination. "So being sent out by the Holy Spirit, they went down to Seleucia, and from there they sailed to Cyprus" (Acts 13:4). They first chose to go to Cyprus. They didn't begin by wandering around in an arbitrary fashion. The Mediterranean island of Cyprus presented a logical destination. It was nearby, only a short sail from the port city of Seleucia. And, more importantly, it was the home country of Barnabas (Acts 4:36). What better place to begin than a place familiar to Barnabas, a place where he would be given a hearing based on his connection with his listeners? Similar opportunities exist for all of us as well.

When Barnabas and Paul arrived in Cyprus, they immediately went to the synagogues and preached: "And when they arrived in Salamis, they preached the word of God in the synagogues of the Jews" (Acts 13:5). Again, we can observe a logical, intentional strategy.

Barnabas and Paul were both Jews and had much in common with the Jews in Cyprus. What better place to quickly and efficiently establish relationships that would afford them opportunities to share their Christian faith? Paul continued this strategy throughout his ministry, as is apparent from their next stop in Asia Minor. We read, "But when they departed from Perga, they came to Antioch in Pisidia, and went into the synagogue on the Sabbath day and sat down" (Acts 13:14).

When identifying potential relationships in order to extend our social network, logical points of contact are important. Sometimes opportunities for new relationships present themselves to us without any action on our part. However, more often than not, a little forethought and intention on our part is required. Once we become proactive about extending our network, opportunities will abound.

Once we have identified some potential relationships, it is up to us to establish these new relationships. Again, we have to be intentional. When Jesus entered Jericho, he encountered a crowd of people who wanted to see him. One man in the crowd, due to his stature, was forced to climb a tree to see him. This man, Zacchaeus, was a notorious tax collector. He was the last person in Jericho with whom anyone would have expected Jesus to socialize. Yet, Jesus noticed him in the tree. "And when Jesus came to the place, He looked up and saw him, and said to him, 'Zacchaeus, make haste and come down, for today I must stay at your house'"

(Luke 19:5). Now, what may seem to us a rather arrogant demand for hospitality on behalf of Jesus was not. Instead, it was a gesture of acceptance. No one in Jericho liked Zacchaeus, who apparently had cheated many of them by collecting excess taxes for his own enrichment. In fact, many heavily criticized Jesus for associating with him, complaining and saying, "'He has gone to be a guest with a man who is a sinner'" (Luke 19:7). Of course, Zacchaeus was converted and as a result sought to make restitution for all he had stolen. "And Jesus said to him, 'Today salvation has come to this house, because he also is a son of Abraham; for the Son of Man has come to seek and to save that which was lost'" (Luke 19:9-10). All this came about because Jesus established an immediate relationship with Zacchaeus when he expressed his desire to lodge at his house. In doing this, he offered Zacchaeus love and acceptance rather than condemnation.

When Jesus first met the woman at the well in Samaria, it was about noon. This was an unusual time for a woman to be drawing water. Women normally came early in the day to draw water. This probably indicates that she was not welcome to associate with the other women. Evidently this was due to her immoral lifestyle since she had been married five times and was currently living with someone who was not her husband (John 4:17). Upon meeting her, Jesus said, "Give Me a drink" (John 4:7). Again, this request sounds like an arrogant demand until we understand it. We must note that Jews as a rule refused to speak to

Samaritans and that Jewish men did not speak to women, even Jewish women, in public. So Jesus offered her immediate respect and acceptance by making this simple request. By this means a relationship with her was established from the outset, and their conversation then led to her personal faith in him as the Messiah.

Sharing our faith should not be thought of as a passive endeavor. Neither should it be left to chance but facilitated by the intentional establishment of a relationship. It may be a relationship that is established almost immediately, as in the cases of Zacchaeus and the woman of Samaria. Sometimes it takes more time and effort.

As part of a rest home ministry that provides a monthly worship service, Louise and another lady made some room-to-room visits one evening and met a ninety-nine-year-old woman. The woman made it clear that she wasn't interested in hearing what they had to say. However, during the brief visit, Louise noticed a Scrabble board the resident had near her and asked if she might return sometime and play with her. This request brought an immediate and affirmative answer, so she began to visit the elderly woman on a regular basis to play Scrabble. After several visits and much prayer, the formerly disinterested woman finally became willing to listen to the gospel message. Similarly, we need to take the time and make the effort to extend our network. New relationships bring unique opportunities, and these God-given opportunities should not be missed.

The Relationship Landscape

Although we need to purposefully extend our network of relationships, we also need to keep in mind that our objective is not to identify only a few spiritually needy individuals to approach while ignoring the rest. We have a responsibility to everyone in our relationship landscape. It is our job to move each and every one of the individuals in our network closer to God. Remember, our responsibility to make disciples can be compared to a game of Sorry! where the object is to be the first to move all four game pieces around the outer edge of the board and into a final safe zone. Our network will be much larger than four game pieces, but our responsibility is the same—to move each individual in our landscape closer to the goal of Christlikeness. Some will need to be introduced to Christ for the first time. Others will already be believers but will still need our spiritual aide in one way or another. We need to purposefully and effectively share our faith with each of them to the best of our ability. All of them are important. This is our commission.

6

NETWORK WORK

Getting Involved

I first witnessed a plate-spinning act many years ago when a small, independent circus came to town. I was fascinated by the performer's ability to keep a large number of plates spinning at one time. The glass dinner plates were set spinning on multiple sticks held vertically in stands about shoulder high. In such acts the performer starts a plate spinning, and it continues to spin on its own for some time due to the gyroscopic effect. More and more spinning plates are added one at a time while keeping all the plates spinning. As additional plates are added, the initial spinning plates begin to lose their momentum and wobble on their sticks. The seemingly frantic performer scurries about in comedic fashion, revisiting the wobbly plates to give them a second spin while continuing to set more and more new plates spinning. Sometimes a plate falls to the stage and shatters. The world record for simultaneously spinning plates stands at 108. Maintaining a large number of significant human relationships is much like spinning 108 plates at one time. It takes constant attention. As new relationships are established, our existing network of relationships must be maintained. In spite of our best efforts, some relationships will cease to function. However, more than necessary will fall off of their stick and shatter on the ground if we become haphazard about maintaining our network of relationships.

A thriving network of relationships takes a lot of work, but it is necessary work. A healthy network of relationships will enable us to share our faith without fear and ultimately make disciples. How do we keep our network of relationships spinning smoothly? The answer is to be continually involved in the lives of the people in our network. We have to get involved and stay involved in the lives of people. Steps three and four to sharing our faith without fear provide two practical ways to get involved.

PRAY PURPOSEFULLY ABOUT MAKING DISCIPLES

Prayer should be a regular and natural part of the Christian life. It is both a personal responsibility and a natural response to our daily struggles and acute needs. As Paul wrote, "Be anxious for nothing, but in everything by prayer and supplication, with thanksgiving, let your requests be made known to God" (Phil. 4:6). We are also compelled to pray about the needs of those we care about. Prayers offered for the benefit of others are called intercessory prayers. Intercession usually includes the following types of general requests: prayer for God's blessing, requests for the resolution of some personal problem or difficulty, petitions for physical health or safety, and requests for the salvation of unbelievers. General intercession tends to be the emphasis of most believers. However, there are only a few examples in the Scriptures. John prayed, "Beloved, I pray that you may prosper in all things and be in health, just as your soul prospers" (3 John 2). And Paul's prayer for Israel was, "Brethren, my heart's desire and prayer to God for Israel is that they may be saved" (Rom. 10:1). In contrast to general intercession, intercession concerned with making disciples requires very specific requests. Although often overlooked in practice, examples of this type of focused intercession are abundant in the Scriptures, and several different categories are identifiable in the New Testament.

A more specific type of intercession is focused on discipleship and involves requests for the edification or spiritual growth of believers. Overwhelmingly, this is the emphasis of Paul's intercession:

- He prayed that the Corinthians might resist temptation (2 Cor. 13:7) and that they might be complete (2 Cor. 13:9).

- He prayed for the church in Philippi that their love might abound (Phil. 1:9).

- He prayed that the church in Colossae might have greater knowledge and wisdom (Col. 1:9).

- He prayed that the Thessalonian church would fulfill God's will (2 Thess. 1:11).

We must keep in mind that a large part of disciple making is the edification of other believers we know.

Therefore, it is understandable that Paul's emphasis was on praying for the edification of others.

Another scriptural emphasis in regard to intercession involves praying for opportunities to share our faith. These include opportunities both to edify fellow believers and to witness to nonbelievers. Biblical examples include the following:

- Paul requested that the Thessalonians pray for him and his team of evangelists that the Word of the Lord would "run swiftly and be glorified" (2 Thess. 3:1). What he desired was an unhindered opportunity for God's Word to accomplish its purpose.

- Paul also urged the Colossians to pray for him and his fellow workers. He asked that they pray for both opportunity and sufficiency: "Continue … praying also for us, that God would open us a door for the word, to speak the mystery of Christ, for which I am also in chains, that I may make it manifest, as I ought to speak" (Col. 4:2-4). Paul's greatest concern during his time of confinement was that a door of opportunity be opened for him to preach the Word and that he may do so effectively.

- God-given opportunity was afforded Paul in Ephesus: "For a great and effectual door has opened to me" (1 Cor. 16:9).

- John tells us that such an open door was also set before the church in Philadelphia: "See, I have set before you an open door, and no one can shut it" (Rev. 3:8).

Undoubtedly, our intercessions should include praying for opportunities. We need to pray specifically for the right opportunity to share our faith with those individuals in our network of relationships. If we develop relationships and pray for opportunities, they will come. Many times they come whether we have specifically prayed for them or not, but if we are praying for opportunities, we are more likely to recognize them when they present themselves, simply because we are expecting them.

Another scriptural emphasis in regard to intercession involves praying for boldness. In the early days of the church in Jerusalem, a great number of conversions took place in response primarily to the preaching of Peter and the other apostles (see Acts 2:41, 47; 4:4). This was unacceptable to the Jewish leaders, who arrested Peter and John and commanded them to speak no more in the name of Jesus (Acts 4:18). Of course, Peter and John replied in no uncertain terms that they would not cease to speak: "But Peter and John answered and said to them, 'Whether it is right in the sight of God to listen to you more than to God, you judge. For we cannot but speak the things which we have seen and heard'" (Acts 4:19-20). In spite of their bold words, there was obviously considerable pressure on them, and all the disciples, to throttle back their public witness. Consequently, they prayed for boldness: "Now, Lord, look on their threats, and grant to your servants that with all boldness they may speak Your word" (Acts 4:29). The Greek word translated "boldness" here is a word that refers to freedom of speech. Freedom of speech was a familiar concept in that day due to the Greek city-states, which granted that right to its citizens. So the believers prayed for an internal liberty to speak, a freedom from intimidation. The answer to their prayer was forthcoming. "And when they had prayed, the place where they were assembled together was shaken; and they were all filled with the Holy Spirit, and spoke the word of God with boldness." (Acts 4:31). We should not confuse the two things mentioned in verse 31. The first, being filled with the Spirit, requires the conscious submission to the Spirit's leading. We are commanded to be filled, or controlled, by the Spirit in Scripture: "And do not be drunk with wine, in which is dissipation; but be filled with the Spirit" (Eph. 5:18). The second, boldness, is something we can request of God—and should. When we do, he will answer our prayers as he did in Acts 4. Note some additional examples:

- Paul was bold in speaking the gospel in Thessalonica as he reminded them later: "But even after we had suffered before and were spitefully treated at Philippi, as you know, we were bold in our God to speak to you the gospel of God in much conflict" (1 Thess. 2:2). As in Acts 4, again boldness was of great importance in evangelizing unbelievers.

- Finally, in Paul's second letter to the Corinthians he mentions boldness in reference to fellow believers in need of edification (2 Cor. 10:1-2).

One final emphasis in Scripture in regard to intercession involves praying for help in the matter of sharing our faith. Note a couple of examples:

- "Then He said to his disciples, 'The harvest truly is plentiful, but the laborers are few. Therefore pray the Lord of the harvest to send our laborers into His harvest'" (Matt. 9:37-38).

- He said the same thing when he sent out the seventy (Luke 10:2). It is always beyond us to reach everyone, and quite often it will be beyond us to reach everyone in our own social network. We need help. We should regularly pray for it.

MEET NEEDS IN YOUR NETWORK

The second practical way to stay involved in the lives of those people who make up our network of relationships is to meet their needs. When we encounter someone who has a need we can meet, it is imperative that we meet that need. Jesus said, "You shall love the Lord your God with all your heart, with all your soul, with all your strength, and with all your mind, and your neighbor as yourself" (Luke 10:27). Unbelieving neighbors are not usually aware of their spiritual needs, and fellow believers are often satisfied with their present level of spiritual growth. However, both are very much aware of any material, physical, or emotional needs they have. Given this reality, it is unlikely they will listen to what we have to say about their spiritual needs, if at the same time we ignore the needs that are so obvious to them. On the other hand, assisting them with their obvious needs will build a foundation upon which we can later address their spiritual needs.

Meeting needs begins with emotional support. Paul wrote, "Rejoice with those who rejoice, and weep with those who weep" (Rom. 12:15). People need someone to rejoice with them when they are blessed and to weep with them when they are hurting. Emotional support is essential to all good relationships. How often do we let envy get in the way of truly rejoicing with others? And how often do we let pride interfere with expressing true sympathy? When someone has experienced the recent loss of a loved one and is wrestling with profound grief, we are often at a loss as to what to say. We might even avoid that person, thinking we have nothing to offer. However, it is not necessary to have all the answers. What is needed is to join with that person in his or her grief as best we can and express our sympathy.

Meeting needs also includes practical help of all kinds, as demonstrated in the following passages:

- The Samaritan provided exactly the help the injured man needed. He rendered medical assistance, provided personal care, transportation, and after arriving at the inn, lodging and ongoing care at his own expense (Luke 10:30-35).

- Meeting practical needs is governed only by our opportunities. As Paul said, "Therefore, as we have opportunity, let us do good to all, especially to those who are of the household of faith" (Gal. 6:10).

- James said, "If a brother or sister is naked and destitute of daily food, and one of you says to them, 'Depart in peace, be warmed and filled,' but do not give them the things which are needed for the body, what does it profit?" (James 2:15-16).

Years ago my wife and I faced a large medical bill that our insurance did not cover. We were making small monthly payments to the hospital when a dear couple in the church I pastored gave us a four-hundred-dollar check toward the debt. That was a huge amount for us in those days. It didn't fully pay off the debt, but it helped a lot. More important, it encouraged our hearts immensely and increased our faith. Sincere love offered to meet real needs pays huge dividends. Of course, we should exclude those who impose on others when it is not necessary. Paul wrote, "For even when we were with you, we commanded you this: If anyone will not work, neither should he eat" (2 Thess. 3:10).

Examples of need-centered love abound in the Scriptures. Zacchaeus and the woman at the well were both social outcasts in need of a friend until they met Jesus. Can you imagine Zacchaeus, the despised tax collector, being allowed to step in front of the crowd that was hoping to see Jesus? Not a soul would have let him through, but Jesus reached out to him in the tree, and it was an avenue to his heart (Luke 19:1-10). A similar example is found in the Gospel of John when Jesus encountered the woman at the well. Her immoral lifestyle was well known. She too was an outcast, but to her surprise Jesus didn't treat her as such. A simple request for a drink of water and a willingness to converse with her opened the door, and she too believed (John 4:1-42).

Peter's encounter with the lame man provides another similar example. Peter and John were on their way to the temple shortly after the events of Pentecost when they came across a lame man asking for a hand- out. Peter did not have the means to help him finan- cially, but he did have the ability to deal with the man's greater problem. "Then Peter said, 'Silver and gold I do not have, but what I do have I give you: In the name of Jesus Christ of Nazareth, rise up and walk'" (Acts 3:6). Because Peter possessed the apostolic gift of healing, the man was instantly healed. Peter met the man's physical need, and his material one as well, since he was now able to work. More importantly, the man's life was changed spiritually. Whereas, before he spent his days begging, now he went about praising God (Acts 3:8-9).

Meeting needs, whether they are emotional or ma- terial, is foundational to addressing a person's deeper spiritual need. However, one warning is necessary when it comes to meeting needs with the intention of making disciples. Our concern for the needs of others must be sincere. Paul said, "Let love be without hypocrisy" (Rom. 12:9). Only sincere concern and heartfelt assistance builds the necessary foundation for addressing spiritual needs. Jesus healed people because he had sincere compassion for them (Matt. 14:14; 20:34), and he fed the hungry multitudes for the same reason (Matt. 15:32). Sincere compassion for the needs of another person is the only benevolence that lays the proper foundation. I love to tell my granddaughter Bible stories, and she is a ready listener, but how effective would I be in helping make her a disciple of Jesus, if I did not also get her a drink of water when she was thirsty or applaud her latest artwork? We would do well to remember the following observation: "If other people think that you only care about who they will become in the future, they will quickly and consistently resist your attempts to connect. They do not want you to look at them as you would a remodeling project, focusing on what things will look like after you 'fix it.'"[17] Certainly, meeting needs lays a foundation for making disciples, but we should sincerely love our neighbors anyway, whether or not anything further comes of it.

Meeting needs may not seem to be that important when compared to actually speaking to a person about their greater need of Christ, but it is a powerful tool and often a necessary aspect of reaching people. For example, my friend Ann works at a job where employees

---

[17] John Townsend, *Loving People* (Nashville: Thomas Nelson, 2008), 91.

are not allowed to speak to anyone about God. Yet, she has had over two dozen fellow workers visit her church in the last eight years as a result of developing relationships with them at work and responding to their needs.

So far we have outlined four steps to sharing our faith without fear. The first two involve taking an inventory of our existing relationships and purposefully seeking to expand that network of relationships. The third and fourth steps covered in this chapter are interceding on behalf of our network and meeting the needs of those included. These four steps are foundational and prepare the way for sharing our faith orally, and they are indispensable. It is adhering to this step-by-step process that will remove most—if not all—of the fear associated with sharing our faith with other people. Therefore, it is always a good idea to follow through on each of these steps in succession with each and every individual in our network of relationships.

7

GET THE MESSAGE OUT

Communicating Our Faith

It was not an unusual request for a pastor to receive. A friend from out of town wanted me to visit a family member who was hospitalized near me. I was more than happy to do so since the man was seriously ill and had not accepted Christ as his Savior. Someone needed to speak to him about his need of Christ, and soon. I hurried to the hospital, determined to address his spiritual condition. He admitted that he was not a believer and listened patiently as I explained the gospel, but he rejected my invitation to place his faith in Christ. Disappointed, I asked him if he would at least think about what we had discussed. He said, "Yes," but I wasn't very optimistic that he would do it. A day or two later I went back to see him again, but he had been discharged. After a week or so, my friend called again to tell me the same man was back in the hospital. Again, I went to see him, this time with more determination than before to see him accept Christ. After exchanging initial pleasantries, I asked him if he had thought about what we had discussed previously. I was pleasantly surprised when he indicated that he had indeed thought about our previous discussion. Emboldened, I promptly headed down the "Romans Road" again, hoping that this time the outcome would be different. Once again, he listened patiently to my detailed and impassioned explanation of the gospel. When I finished, I eagerly asked him if he would now like to accept Christ as his Savior. A man of few words, he simply replied as before, "No." My hope instantly turned into frustration, and I blurted out, "Why not?" Again, in nonchalant fashion he gave me a simple answer: "I've already done that." Between my two visits, at the Holy Spirit's prompting, he had come to faith in Christ. I do not know why he let me go through the gospel in detail that second time without stopping me. Stunned and a little embarrassed is the only way to characterize my reaction at the time. In retrospect, the whole episode is somewhat humorous, but the truths highlighted by the events of that day are indelibly etched into my mind. We are never any more than messengers. We cannot by any effort or argument of our own convince anyone to place his or her faith in Christ. Only the Holy Spirit can do that, and we have to leave it to him.

Thus far we have outlined four steps to sharing our faith without fear. The first two steps involve taking an inventory of our existing relationships and purposefully seeking to expand that network of relationships. The third and fourth steps are interceding for those in our network and meeting their needs. These four steps provide the necessary foundation for completing the task, but we also have to communicate our faith perspective in order to effectively share what we believe. It is speaking to others about our faith that often evokes enough fear to inhibit us. However, if we have laid the necessary relational foundation, speaking to someone about our faith should not intimidate us. In fact, if the right approach is utilized, anyone can share his or her faith without fear. All that has to be done is to add the two final steps that are needed to effectively complete the process.

DELIVER THE MESSAGE

The fifth step in the process of sharing our faith without fear is to consistently inform others of our faith-based perspective on their needs. In the context of someone's spiritual need and on the basis of an established relationship with the person involved, we should be able to deliver the appropriate faith-based message naturally and without fear. Although discipleship is always the ultimate goal, the message we deliver will vary from person to person. It is determined by the need of the recipient, and we have to deliver the right message.

Unbelievers in our social network require a totally different message than fellow believers. First and foremost, they require a salvation message. Our job is to deliver the gospel message to them. The power to reach the lost resides in the message of the gospel we deliver. Paul wrote, "For I am not ashamed of the gospel of Christ, for it is the power of God to salvation for everyone who believes, for the Jew first and also for the Greek" (Rom. 1:16). Where there is saving faith, it is always the result of hearing God's message of salvation. "So then faith comes by hearing, and hearing by the word of God" (Rom. 10:17).

The timing of our witness to nonbelievers is also important. It is important because they are not always ready to listen. It is also important because the right timing will further eliminate any fear we may have of delivering the gospel message. It will not be forced upon someone who is not ready but delivered to someone who is ready to receive it. God will grant us such opportunities from time to time, and we need to seize them. Examples abound in Scripture.

- What seems like a coincidence can be providential. Jesus encountered the Samaritan woman at Jacob's well at an odd time—noonday. With his disciples having been sent into town and her visit to the well coming at a solitary time, Jesus was able to hold a private conversation with her, a conversation that led to her eternal salvation (John 4:5-43).

- What seems like an imposition can be an opportunity. When Paul and Silas were imprisoned in Philippi, they sang praises to God that evidently were overheard by the jailer. Later when an earthquake made the escape of all the prisoners possible yet they did not flee, the jailer was so impacted that he was converted (Acts 16:23-31).

- What seems pointless can be a sovereign appointment for us to speak with those who will respond to the gospel, as it was in Corinth for Paul (Acts 18:9-11).

- What seems to be an interruption of our plans can be an opportunity to fulfill God's will. We have to pay the price associated with taking advantage of an opportunity to evangelize an unbeliever, redeeming or purchasing the time (Col. 4:5-6).

- What seems like a challenge or a criticism can be an important moment to explain what we believe to a skeptical person (2 Pet. 3:15).

The right time to deliver the gospel message often comes at an unexpected moment. Such was the case when Dorothy happened upon a man she often saw in the course of her daily work. He knew of her faith from previous conversations, but she didn't know where he stood with the Lord. This particular day he was dealing with a serious problem and needed to talk to someone. Dorothy's arrival was providential. Emphatically, he complained, "I don't know why all this is happening to me. I'm not a bad person." And then he added, "I hope I make it to heaven." His words were an expression of frustration, but they were also an open invitation for Dorothy to explain the good news of God's grace and the assurance it provides. A door of opportunity unexpectedly opened that day—a garage-door-sized opportunity—and Dorothy quickly took advantage of it. So should we, whenever God opens a door.

The content of the message we deliver at any point in time will vary in its extent, depending on the situation. There are three levels of faith-based communication, each one being more extensive and to the point than the previous. A level-one message is any "personal statement" we make in public, verbal or nonverbal, about who we are. These statements might include such things as Christian artwork displayed in our home, bumper stickers that reference our faith, Christmas decorations such as a manger scene adorning our property, Facebook posts or e-mail footer messages that include Scripture, grace offered before meals in public, wearing Christian jewelry or T-shirts, and many other similar expressions of our faith.

A level-two message is any "purposeful statement" we make about what we believe. These messages include statements we make in our daily conversations, opinions we offer on various topics, declarations we make about what we believe is true, specific answers we give to questions we receive, and any requested advice or counsel we give. These statements may or may not touch on the gospel, but they communicate some aspect of God's truth nonetheless.

A level-three message is any "plain presentation" of the gospel that we make to another person or persons. This can be a one-on-one presentation that we make in response to a question about what we believe. It can be a presentation we initiate when we perceive someone is willing to listen. It can be a presentation given to a group at a home Bible study or church service. A presentation of the gospel will include man's need of salvation due to his sin, God's provision of a Savior who died in man's place, and the necessity of faith as the means of appropriating salvation. A gospel presentation such as the venerable "Romans Road" should be memorized, carried in tract form, or downloaded to a smart phone. The delivery of any faith-based message is important, but the delivery of a level-three message is the goal. Certainly, a level-three message can be delivered more than once, but we need to keep in mind that we are not responsible for anything more than its delivery.

Finally, when evangelizing unbelievers, our expectations need to be realistic. The reality is that most individuals will not accept Christ as their Savior. Jesus plainly stated that "many" will follow the broad road to eternal destruction and that "few" will travel the narrow road to eternal life (Matt. 7:13-14). Moreover, in the parable of the sower, only one of the four seeds sown by the sower took root, grew, and produced fruit (Matt. 13:3-8). Only the fruitful plant that received the word of the kingdom (the seed) into the good ground (the heart) truly understood the message and received it (Matt. 13:23). The rest—the majority—were false professors (Matt. 13:18-22). Furthermore, whatever one's view of election may be, it is clear that the elect are chosen from out of a larger group (Eph. 1:3-7). Finally, it is clear that the phenomenal expansion of the early church recorded in the book of Acts was due in large part to the miraculous signs performed by the apostles.

Certainly, it is not realistic for us to anticipate the same success in reaching the lost.

During my seminary days I attended a small church that was associated with a larger church in the area. Our church didn't have a visitation program like the mother church, so a fellow classmate and I decided to do some door-to-door evangelism on our own in the neighborhoods surrounding the church. Admittedly, I was uneasy about it, but as far as we knew that's the way evangelism was supposed to be done in those days. We told the pastor, who was one of our seminary instructors, about our plans. That was many years ago, but I still remember what he said. I remember it so vividly because it was not what I expected to hear. Although "winning souls" was a huge emphasis at the seminary we attended, he steered our thinking in a different direction. He said, "Remember, God is glorified when we tell people about Christ whether or not they accept him." Instead of cheering us on or commending us for our initiative, he was more concerned about sparing us from disappointment and the feelings of failure that might follow.

For most of us there will be more fellow believers in our social network than there will be unbelievers. We are also responsible for helping to disciple them. We will have more opportunities to "adopt" disciples than we will ever have to be part of the birth process. When it comes to fellow believers, our focus should be on their edification. Every believer has the responsibility to edify fellow believers. Ephesians 4:11-12 tells us, "And

He Himself gave some to be apostles, some prophets, some evangelists, and some pastors and teachers for the equipping of the saints for the work of the ministry for the edifying of the body of Christ." The construction of verse 11 indicates that four local church offices are in view. "Apostles" and "prophets" were foundational offices and thus were temporary (see Eph. 2:20). This leaves the two permanent offices of "evangelists" and "pastors and teachers." The pastor-teacher office has the primary role of equipping the church. The Greek word translated "equipping" means to supply or furnish what is lacking. Once the saints are equipped, they are to do the "work of the ministry." The work of the ministry is specified to be the "edifying of the body of Christ." The Greek word translated "edifying" means to construct, build, or build up something. This means that every member of the body of Christ has a ministry responsibility of building up other members in the faith. This responsibility is to be equated with the responsibility of "teaching them to observe all things that I have commanded you," as stated in the Great Commission (Matt. 28:20).

Fellow believers are often stymied in their spiritual growth, remaining babes in Christ (1 Cor. 3:1-3) who still need to be instructed at a time when they should be instructing others (Heb. 5:12). Individual believers can most effectively do the work of edification by utilizing their spiritual gift(s) (see Rom. 12:3-8; 1 Cor. 12:1-31). Some of the spiritual gifts enumerated in the New Testament were clearly temporary sign-gifts. Others such as ministry, helping, mercy, leading, administrating, giving, exhorting, and teaching are still operative in the body of Christ, and all specify certain areas of giftedness or expertise usable for edifying the body. Even more basic is the responsibility to use our words constructively to edify others (Eph. 4:29).

INVEST IN THE PROCESS

In financial circles a "trader" is someone who is constantly buying and selling stocks, bonds, or other financial assets. A trader seeks to buy as low as possible and sell a little higher as soon as his position will net a reasonable profit. He never holds anything for very long. In contrast, an "investor" buys and holds a financial asset over a long period of time, ignoring the day-to-day price swings. He hopes to make a reasonable gain one day in the future. He counts on the tendency of the market to appreciate over time. Although some approach making disciples like a trader does financial assets, making disciples is not a series of brief encounters. Success rarely comes quickly for disciple makers. Making a spiritual impact in another person's life requires an investment, an investment in the process of making disciples. This is the sixth step in sharing our faith without fear.

Reaching unbelievers is a process that takes time and patience. The theological basis for this is clear in the Scriptures, although it isn't always recognized. The process of making disciples is dependent upon the Holy Spirit, of whom Jesus said, "When He is come, He will convict the world of sin, and of righteousness, and of judgment" (John 16:8). The word translated "convict" means to convince. Contrary to oft-used terminology drawn from Proverbs, we do not "win souls" to Christ. Soul winning is the Holy Spirit's job, and he does it on his timetable. Professions of faith are the end result of the process. Without the work of the Spirit, unbelievers would not believe, for "the natural man does not receive the things of the Spirit of God, for they are foolishness to him; nor can he know them, because they are spiritually discerned" (1 Cor. 2:14). The natural man is subject to the blinding power of Satan. Paul wrote, "But even if our gospel be veiled, it is veiled to those who are perishing, whose minds the god of this age has blinded, who do not believe, lest the light of the gospel of the glory of Christ, who is the image of God, should shine on them" (2 Cor. 4:3-4). Only the Holy Spirit can penetrate spiritual darkness.

Jesus used the process of sowing and reaping to illustrate the disciple-making process (John 4:35). Sowing is done early in the growing season, and reaping comes at the end. It is a process. Both the sowers and the reapers will be rewarded equally for their part in the process (John 4:36).

Multiple scriptural examples confirm that coming to Christ is the result of an ongoing process. It may be a fairly short process, or a longer one.

- Nicodemus came to Christ and heard the message of salvation (John 3:3), but the Scriptures do not indicate that he acted on it at that time. Then, later, Nicodemus assisted Joseph, a colleague on the Sanhedrin who is specifically identified as a secret believer, in the burial of Jesus (John 19:38-39). It seems that Nicodemus also had become a believer sometime after first talking to Jesus. Exactly how much time passed between the two events is unknown, but Nicodemus's conversion obviously wasn't instantaneous upon first talking to Jesus.

- The woman of Samaria came to faith as the result of a single conversation with Christ. However, Jesus first established a friendly relationship with her and then patiently dealt with her need and addressed her objections (John 4:5-26). Her conversion did not require a long process, but it was a process nonetheless.

- The converts at Pentecost who responded in faith after hearing Peter's sermon (Acts 2:41) were first impacted by the miracle of tongues as each heard the apostles' message in his own dialect (Acts 2:5-12). It was a short process, but clearly a sequence of events was involved.

- The Ethiopian eunuch responded quickly to Philip's explanation of Isaiah's prophecy, but he had been reading the Word of God prior to that, and it is not known for how long (Acts 8:26-38).

- The Philippian jailer specifically asked for information on how to be saved (Acts 16:30), but he had obviously heard much from Paul and Silas already. Also, in addition to having heard them both praying and singing hymns to God in the night (Acts 16:25), he was impacted by the earthquake that freed the prisoners and the fact that all still remained (Acts 16:26-27). Obviously, his conversion was the result of a somewhat short, but very powerful, sequence of events.

- When the apostle Paul described his conversion experience to King Agrippa, he related the message he received from the Lord after he had fallen to the ground: "Saul, Saul, why are you persecuting Me? It is hard for you to kick against the goads" (Acts 26:14). The Lord compared what the Holy Spirit was doing in Paul's heart to prodding animals along with a sharp stick. This process of conviction carried on by the Holy Spirit probably began when Paul heard Stephen's testimony (Acts 6:8–7:60) and concluded on the Damascus road sometime later (Acts 9:1-6).

Here's an example of the process involved in reaching an unbeliever using the relational method. Suzanne decided to extend her network of relationships while doing her weekly grocery shopping. After praying for an opportunity to present itself, she noticed a particular employee who had a sad disposition. When it came time to check out, she chose his checkout aisle, and while checking out, she asked him how he was doing. He responded that he was not doing well and had in fact just become homeless. This led to a brief opportunity for her to share with him how the Lord had carried her through a difficult time in her life. Each week thereafter she chose his checkout aisle, faithfully listened to his concerns, and promised to pray for him. In this way a new and purposeful relationship was established. After some time, she wrote him a letter explaining the gospel and encouraging him to place his faith in Christ. The next time she did her grocery shopping, she asked him if he had read the letter. He affirmed that he had and proceeded to converse with her about his need of Christ until he had to move on to the next customer. Before leaving the checkout aisle that day, Suzanne arranged to meet him on his break to finish the conversation. A short time later on a bench outside the store, her new friend placed his faith in Christ as his Savior.

Edifying those who are already believers is also a process that requires time and patience. No one ever achieves perfect Christlikeness. The apostle Paul never did. He wrote, "Not that I have already attained, or am already perfected; but I press on, that I may lay hold of that for which Christ Jesus has also laid hold of me" (Phil. 3:10). Spiritual growth is a lifelong process, and we need each other's help over and over again. Mutual edification is constantly required. We have to remain invested in the process.

If utilized, the six-step relational model should enable us to share our faith without surrendering to fear. However, it does not guarantee wildly successful results. What we are able to accomplish may seem meager. Few of us will ever become a highly successful disciple maker like Bill Bright, who founded Campus Crusade for Christ. However, we can all be invested in the process like Edward Kimball was. Kimball would be totally unknown to us today, if not for one person he led to Christ.

> A 19th century Sunday school teacher named Kimball led a shoe clerk named Moody to Jesus Christ. Moody became a famous evangelist who influenced Frederick B. Meyer to preach on college campuses. Meyer led J. Wilbur Chapman to the Lord. Chapman while working with the YMCA arranged for Billy Sunday to come to Charlotte, North Carolina to attend revival meetings. Impressed, community leaders in Charlotte scheduled another revival with Mordecai Hamm. Under Hamm's preaching Billy Graham gave his heart to Jesus Christ. Billy Graham has preached to more people than any other man in history. I am sure this Sunday school teacher in Boston had no idea what would happen from leading the shoe clerk to Christ.[18]

---

[18] Jim Borror, *Countdown* (Long Beach, CA: March 2000), 1.

What we accomplish by sharing our faith may seem meager, but only God knows what may be the multiplied results.

Six Steps to Sharing Your Faith Without Fear

1. Inventory your relationships
2. Extend your network
3. Pray purposely about making disciples
4. Meet needs in your network
5. Deliver the message
6. Invest in the process

8

MIND OVER CHATTER

Becoming a Confident Messenger

Jerry Lynch was a professional baseball player who played for the Pittsburgh Pirates and Cincinnati Reds from 1954 through 1966. Lynch was a career reserve outfielder, but he was noted for his pinch-hitting ability. A *pinch hitter* in baseball is someone who is called upon to hit for another player, usually a pitcher who is not a good hitter. Many times the pinch hitter is called on at the most critical juncture of the game and whether or not he comes through with a base hit often impacts the final outcome. Jerry Lynch came through as a pinch hitter 116 times during his thirteen-year career. Having grown up in the Ohio Valley, I still remember radio announcers and others referring to Lynch's appearances as "Lynch in a pinch." This is what Jerry Lynch had to say about the art of pinch-hitting: "The good pinch-hitter is a guy who can relax enough to get a good pitch he can hit. You almost always do get one pitch to hit every time you bat. So you have to have the patience to wait."[19] In other words a good pinch-hitter is confident enough in his ability to relax, be patient, and wait for the right pitch. He can't be anxious or impatient and be successful. Confidence makes a huge difference in our ability to handle any high-pressure situation.

Whenever someone indicates he or she is ready to consider accepting Christ as Savior, it is an exciting moment, but it can also be a moment of profound apprehension and self-doubt. A person for whom we feel responsible stands ready to make the most important decision he or she will ever make. Will the person respond to our message or reject it. The person's eternal destiny hangs in the balance. Given the significance of the moment, it is not unusual to feel inadequate or unqualified to proceed. However, we need not give in to such feelings. All it takes is the confidence to speak and a clear understanding of the message we need to communicate. How do we develop confidence? It's a matter of adjusting our attitudes and increasing our knowledge. Specifically, there are three important aspects to being a confident and effective communicator of the gospel.

AN ATTITUDE OF DEPENDENCE

Although there is a lot riding on the outcome any time we communicate the gospel, there is no reason to be

---

[19] Cincinnati Reds Hall of Fame and Museum, "Jerry Lynch," http://mlb.mlb.com/cin/hof/

overcome by fear. No one's eternal salvation rests on the ability of the human witness involved. Obviously, we should do our best to communicate the gospel, but it is the work of the Holy Spirit that secures the decision. We have to depend on him. He alone can convince people to believe on Christ. Jesus himself stated, "Nevertheless I tell you the truth. It is to your advantage that I go away; for if I do not go away, the Helper will not come to you; but if I depart, I will send Him to you. And when He has come, He will convict the world of sin, and of righteousness, and of judgment" (John 16:7-8). The "Helper" Jesus spoke of is the person of the Holy Spirit. The Greek word translated "convict" means to convince. So, it is the Holy Spirit's power and not our effort that convinces people to place their faith in Christ. Therefore, we do not need to be concerned about saying the right thing at the right time or making the perfect argument to convince someone to accept Christ. Convincing people to believe is not our responsibility. Embracing this reality frees us to speak confidently.

Our dependence on the Holy Spirit is all the more necessary in today's world, given the widespread dissemination of evolutionary theory. Today an ever-increasing number of individuals reject the biblical concept of creation and deny any accountability to a creator. Often the first hurdle we have to clear with people is establishing that they are accountable to God their Creator (Gen. 2:7; Col. 1:16). This vital premise has to be embraced before anyone responds to the message of salvation. Only the Holy Spirit can enlighten a darkened mind in such cases (2 Cor. 4:3-4). A good way to preface any attempt to explain the message of salvation is simply to ask people whether or not they believe in God and recognize any accountability to him. If they do, we can proceed to a fuller explanation of the gospel. If they do not, perhaps we should leave it to the Holy Spirit to change their minds. Either way, the outcome is ultimately in God's hands.

THE MINDSET OF A MESSENGER

We are called to be messengers—not salesmen and not debaters. This is the second realization that will help us be effective communicators of the gospel. Our responsibility is simply to deliver the message of God's grace. It is not within our power to do more. However, there is power in the message we deliver. Paul said, "For I am not ashamed of the gospel of Christ, for it is the power of God to salvation for everyone who believes, for the Jew first and also for the Greek" (Rom. 1:16). The realization that the power of God rests in the message we deliver as well as the work of the Holy Spirit is liberating. If we simply communicate the message, we have done our part. The gospel itself, along with the conviction of the Holy Spirit, is powerful enough to do the rest. Our part in reaching the lost is merely giving voice to the message. Paul compared this to planting seeds when he wrote, "Who then is Paul, and who is Apollos, but ministers through whom you believed, as the Lord gave to each one? I planted, Apollos watered, but God gave the increase. So then neither he who plants is anything, nor he who waters, but God who gives the increase. Now he who plants and he who waters are one, and each one will receive his own reward according to his own labor" (1 Cor. 3:5-8). We merely plant the seed—the Word of God. Others may come along and water the seeds we plant, but in the end, it is always God who produces the harvest.

A GRASP OF THE CONTENT

If you do not enjoy negotiating, then buying an automobile can be an unpleasant experience. Most buyers are easy pickings for an automobile dealer simply because they are not professional negotiators. On the other hand, the dealer is a professional. At least the sales manager is. Until I got used to the process, it always annoyed me to be passed off to the sales manager after I had spent an hour or more negotiating with the salesman. Suddenly, I would become uncomfortable. Whatever relationship I had developed with the salesman was no longer important.

Unbelievers will likely have the same kind of negative reaction, if they are passed off to someone they don't know after finally expressing an interest in hearing the gospel message. It may relieve insecure believers to call in a perceived expert such as a pastor, but it might also cause unnecessary apprehension for the hearer. The best person to communicate the gospel to someone is usually the one with whom the person already has a relationship—someone who has earned the person's trust. We certainly do not need to call in an expert. As previously noted, we already have the expert help of the Holy Spirit (John 16:7-8) and a powerful message to deliver (Rom. 1:16). The truth is, it really doesn't matter who the human messenger is as long as the message is accurately delivered. Nevertheless, the human messenger does have an important responsibility. He or she has to communicate the truth. As Paul said, "How then shall they call on Him in whom they have not believed? And how shall they believe in Him of whom they have not heard? And how shall they hear without a preacher" (Rom. 10:14)? Even though communicating the message is important, it is not overly difficult. All that is required is an understanding of the message and the confidence to articulate it. The following paragraphs provide an analysis of the message we need to communicate—what is often called the plan of salvation. It may be summarized in three simple points: the need of salvation, the basis of salvation, and the condition of salvation.

The Need of Salvation

Man's need of salvation is the result of his sin and the judgment of God that accompanies it. However, most unbelievers do not recognize their lost condition. There is an old saying that goes something like this: "It is not as difficult to convince people that they need to be saved as it is to convince them that they are lost in the first place." This has never been truer than it is in today's postmodern culture. Today it often takes a great deal of time and patience to successfully communicate such an unpopular truth. As a result, it is often necessary to repeatedly touch on the subject of sin and God's judgment over a period of time, while allowing the Holy Spirit to work. This is best accomplished by simply stating what we believe when we have the opportunity, without making personal accusations or pronouncements of judgment on an individual. The Spirit's conviction in regard to a person's sinfulness cannot be hurried along by our insistence that the listener is a sinner. The Holy Spirit sets his own timetable. Furthermore, premature appeals for immediate decisions will likely be unproductive and may close the door to any future discussion of the matter. However, when we sense that someone is ready to listen, God's Word must be thoroughly and accurately communicated. The following summarizes the need of salvation that we must communicate to unbelievers.

No one meets Gods standard of righteousness. Although one person may exceed another person's righteousness, no one except God is completely righteous (Rom. 3:10). All have sinned and continue to sin against God (Rom. 3:23).

God's judgment for sin is death—physical and spiritual death (Gen. 2:15-17). The judgment of physical death will be remedied at the resurrection of believers (1 Thess. 4:13-18). Spiritual death—defined as spiritual separation from God—is remedied upon the new birth (John 3:1-5; Eph. 2:1-9). Separation from God that is not remedied will become an eternal reality at the Great White Throne Judgment (Rev. 20:11-15).

The Basis of Salvation

The basis of salvation rests in the substitutionary death and resurrection of Jesus Christ. His death and resurrection made it possible for a lost world of sinful people to be saved from eternal judgment.

Jesus Christ died in our place. Christ is the only qualified Savior of mankind. The term *Christ* in the Greek means "the anointed one" and is equivalent to the Old Testament term *Messiah*. The Bible makes clear that the Anointed One is divine (John 1:1, 14; 10:30-33; 20:28; Heb. 1:8). Being God, he was without any sin of his own for which payment was due. At the same time, he was fully human (John 8:40; 1 Tim. 2:5) and thus could serve as man's substitute (1 Cor. 15:3). In death he took upon himself the penalty of mankind's sin (Rom. 4:25; 5:8; 1 Cor. 15:3; 2 Cor. 5:21).

Having paid the price of sin, Christ rose from the dead (1 Cor. 15:4). His resurrection is a necessary part of the gospel because it proves that payment for our sin has been made in full (John 19:30). He rose because of our justification—because He had completed what needed to be done for our justification before God (Rom. 4:25). The Greek word consistently translated "justified" in the New Testament means "declared righteous" or "declared not guilty." God can justly do this based on Christ's death on our behalf.

The Condition of Salvation

The condition of salvation is faith in the Lord Jesus Christ. The Greek word translated "faith" is sometimes translated "believe."

Faith is the one condition to salvation (John 3:16; Rom. 5:1; Eph. 2:8-9). As clear as it may be to us, it is always important to emphasize that human effort plays no role in an individual's salvation. There is no way to make up for our sin. No amount of good works will ever suffice. Salvation is received by faith alone.

True saving faith includes believing the historical facts of Christ's death and resurrection as well as trusting in what he has done to save us, but it also involves accepting him personally as our Lord (Rom. 10:9-10). This means accepting the person of Christ for who he is—the living, resurrected, Lord of all—and giving him our allegiance (Matt. 7:21-23; John 1:12). A saving relationship with Christ requires what the Scripture calls repentance (Luke 13:3; Acts 17:30). To repent literally means to change one's mind. Biblically, it is a change of mind about Christ and one's relationship to him that recognizes his lordship over our lives. We will never be able to perfectly follow Christ as Lord of our life this side of eternity, but he has to be accepted as our rightful Lord. Then and only then is anyone truly saved and able to grow in Christlikeness.

The message of salvation explained above is not beyond the average Christian's ability to understand or communicate. It may take a little study to thoroughly digest it. It would also be good to memorize the key verses. However, it is not that difficult to master, and with mastery comes the confidence to share it.

You never know when an opportunity to share the gospel will arise. A number of years ago my family and I visited Mall of America in Minneapolis. While my wife was shopping and my daughter was riding the indoor roller coaster, I was sitting on a nearby bench. As I sat there with no thought of anything but relaxation on my mind, I was joined by a young man. He was wearing a long trench coat and was obviously distraught. He needed to talk, and I guess I was the only unoccupied person available. He poured out his heart to me over several minutes. Every once in a while, he would reach inside his coat, pull out a bottle of gin, and take a sip. He seemed to have some serious and ongoing family problems. That morning he had stormed off in the midst of an argument with his father and wound up at the mall. However, it wasn't difficult to discern that his most basic need was spiritual. I knew I would probably never see him again and that this would likely be the only opportunity I would ever have to tell him about Christ. I didn't have a Bible with me or even a tract to give to him. There was no one I knew in Minneapolis to whom I could refer him. It was up to me. He listened carefully as I explained his need of salvation and presented the gospel message. I would like to report that he made a decision for Christ, but he did not. He only promised to give my words some thought. He was, however, very appreciative and gave my daughter a sterling silver pendant that he said he got from a store downstairs—by what means I do not know. I can only hope that our conversation led him to Christ. Thankfully, I had the plan of salvation memorized, and I could quote the verses to which I referred. We cannot predict when opportunities to share the good news will come or how. All we can do is be ready and confident enough to follow through.

Made in the USA
Columbia, SC
06 July 2021